Sacred Journeys:

Spiritual Awakening Across Four Continents

Stanley Scott Jr.

■ Sacred Journeys: Spiritual Awakening Across Four Continents

First Edition, October 2024
ISBN: 979-8-9914773-7-6 (Ebook)
ISBN: 979-8-9914773-8-3 (Paperback)

Cover design by Stanley Scott Jr
Interior design by Stanley Scott Jr
Edited by Stanley Scott Jr

Printed in the United States of America

BySScott (Publisher)
Oakland,California 94621
Bysscott.org

This is a work of non-fiction. Names, characters, places, and incidents are real and not fictitious. Any resemblance to actual persons, living or dead, events, or locales are entirely true.

Sacred Journeys: Spiritual Awakening Across Four Continents

■■ Table of Contents

■ Prologue: The Call to Adventure

As I stood on the deck of my San Francisco home, gazing out at the vast expanse of the Pacific Ocean, I felt a stirring in my soul. The rhythmic crashing of waves against the shore seemed to whisper ancient secrets, calling me to lands unknown. It was in this moment that I realized my journey—a journey of spiritual discovery and personal growth—was about to begin.

For years, I had been deeply involved in my work with the ILWU Local 10, fighting for workers' rights and striving to make a difference in my community. But there was another battle I had been fighting, one that had nearly cost me everything: the battle against addiction. In 2011, I found my way into the rooms of Alcoholics Anonymous, marking the beginning of a transformative journey in recovery.

Now, three years into my sobriety, I felt a calling to expand my horizons, to seek out new experiences that would deepen my spiritual understanding and strengthen my recovery. The idea of traveling to distant lands, not as an escape but as a pilgrimage of sorts, began to take root in my mind.

It was then that I remembered the words of the great Maya Angelou: "Perhaps travel cannot prevent bigotry, but by demonstrating that all peoples cry, laugh, eat, worry, and die, it can introduce the idea that if we try and understand each other, we may even become friends." These words resonated deeply within me, igniting a spark of curiosity and wonder that would lead me on an incredible journey across four continents.

My path would take me to four distinct destinations, each with its own unique energy and spiritual significance:

1. Cancun and Chichén Itzá, Mexico - where ancient Mayan wisdom echoes through time
2. Punta Cana, Dominican Republic - where Caribbean rhythms pulse with resilience
3. Durban, South Africa - where unity flourishes in diversity

4. Honolulu, Hawaii - where the Aloha spirit embodies harmony with nature

Little did I know that these four places, seemingly unconnected, would weave together a fabric of spiritual awakening and personal transformation. Each destination would offer its own lessons, its own challenges, and its own moments of profound insight.

As I embarked on this journey, I carried with me the strength and values instilled in me by my parents, my experiences in the labor movement, and the spiritual principles I had learned in recovery. I was about to discover how these foundations would be tested, reinforced, and expanded through my encounters with ancient civilizations, diverse cultures, and the awe-inspiring power of nature.

This book is not just a travelogue, but a testament to the transformative power of travel when undertaken with an open heart and a seeking spirit. It's an exploration of how God's handiwork is manifested in different corners of the world, and how the resilience of people across cultures can inspire us to push forward in our own lives and recovery journeys.

Throughout these travels, I would find myself drawn to moments of prayer and meditation, often near bodies of water. From the beaches of Cancun to the Indian Ocean in Durban, from the Caribbean shores of Punta Cana to the Pacific waters of Hawaii, these moments of spiritual connection would become cornerstones of my journey, deepening my conscious contact with my Higher Power and reinforcing my commitment to recovery.

As we set off on this journey together, I invite you to open your mind to the possibilities that lie ahead. For in the story of my travels, you may find echoes of your own spiritual journey, your own quest for meaning, and your own path to personal growth and recovery.

Let us begin our sacred journey, stepping into the unknown with faith, curiosity, and a willingness to be transformed by the wonders that await us. Whether you're in recovery yourself, curious about different cultures, or simply seeking inspiration,

I hope that my experiences will offer you insight, hope, and the courage to embark on your own journey of discovery.

Remember, as we say in the rooms of recovery, "More will be revealed." So let's turn the page and see where this adventure takes us, one day at a time.

■ Chapter 1: Cancun and Chichén Itzá - Echoes of Ancient Wisdom and Modern Recovery

As the plane touched down in Cancun in 2014, I felt a mix of excitement and trepidation. This trip marked not only the beginning of my spiritual journey across four continents but also a significant milestone in my recovery. For three years, I had been walking the path of sobriety with Alcoholics Anonymous, and this trip to Mexico was a testament to how far I had come.

The morning after our arrival, I found myself attending Mass with Regina Haugebook at a local church. The familiar rhythms of the service, spoken in a language I didn't understand but in a faith I knew well, grounded me. It reminded me of the universal nature of spirituality, transcending language and culture.

Later that day, I attended a 12-step meeting in Cancun. Sitting in a circle with strangers who instantly felt like family, I was struck by the power of shared experience. Despite our different backgrounds, we were united in our struggle and our commitment to recovery. As I shared my story and listened to others, I felt a deep sense of gratitude for the three years of sobriety that had brought me to this point.

The next day, we ventured to the ancient Mayan city of Chichén Itzá. As I stood before the towering Temple of Kukulcán (Pyramid of El Castillo) I couldn't help but draw parallels between the enduring nature of these stone structures and the resilience required in recovery. Just as these pyramids had withstood centuries of weathering and change, so too had I weathered the storms of addiction to stand here, sober and present.

Staring up the steep steps of Kukulkan, each one seemed to represent a step in my recovery journey. Reaching a platform halfway up, I paused to catch my breath and reflect. The 12 steps of AA had been my stairway to a better life, each one challenging but ultimately leading me higher.

As my eyes reached the summit, I was struck by a profound sense of energy and connection - to the earth beneath my feet, to the sky above, and to a power greater than myself. This connection, which I had first discovered through AA and which had kept me sober for three years, felt amplified in this ancient place of spiritual significance.

As I explored the rest of Chichén Itzá, I was continually amazed by the Mayans' deep connection to the natural world and the cosmos. Their understanding of celestial cycles and their integration of spiritual beliefs into everyday life resonated with my own journey of recovery. In AA, I had learned to seek a daily reprieve from addiction through conscious contact with a higher power, much as the Mayans had sought to align their lives with the rhythms of the universe.

That evening, I found myself on the beach in Cancun, watching the sun sink into the Caribbean. As the sky transformed into a canvas of vibrant colors, I closed my eyes and prayed. I thanked my higher power for another day of sobriety, for the strength to make this journey, and for the wisdom I was gaining along the way. The gentle lapping of waves against the shore seemed to echo the serenity prayer that had become such an integral part of my recovery: "God, grant me the serenity to accept the things I cannot change, courage to change the things I can, and wisdom to know the difference."

The next day, we visited the ruins of Tulum, perched dramatically on cliffs overlooking the turquoise waters of the Caribbean. Again, I found myself moved to prayer, grateful for the beauty surrounding me and the clear mind with which I could appreciate it. Standing there, I reflected on the importance of the annual sobriety chip I received in AA. Each year clean was a victory, a testament to the transformative power of the 12-step program and the grace of a higher power.

As I left Cancun and Chichén Itzá behind, I carried with me not just memories of ancient pyramids and beautiful beaches, but a renewed commitment to my recovery journey. The wisdom of the ancient Mayans had reinforced the lessons I'd learned in AA: the importance of connecting with something greater than oneself, of living in harmony with the world around us, and of approaching each day with humility and gratitude.

Little did I know then that this was just the beginning. In the years to come, my recovery journey would evolve, leading me to Narcotics Anonymous in 2020 and to meetings in Hawaii, both online and in person. Each new destination on my travels would bring fresh insights, deepening my spiritual awakening and strengthening my resolve to stay on the path of recovery.

As I boarded the plane for my next destination, I felt a sense of excitement and anticipation. The journey had only just begun, both in terms of my travels and my ongoing recovery. I was eager to see what lessons awaited me, what new spiritual awakenings I would experience, and how each new place would contribute to my growth in sobriety and in life.

■ Chapter 2: Punta Cana - Caribbean Rhythms of Resilience

As the plane descended towards Punta Cana in 2016, the shimmering turquoise waters of the Caribbean came into view, a stark contrast to the ancient stone structures of Chichén Itzá I had explored two years prior. This trip held a special significance for me - not only was I continuing my spiritual journey across continents, but I was also celebrating 5 years of sobriety and sharing this milestone with my fiancée, Venecia Margarita.

The moment we stepped off the plane, the warm Caribbean air enveloped us, carrying with it the promise of new experiences and insights. Little did I know that this trip would offer a profound lesson in love, commitment, and the enduring power of human connection.

Our first evening in Punta Cana, we decided to take a sunset stroll along the beach. As we walked hand in hand, the sand warm beneath our feet and the sky awash with vibrant hues of orange and pink, we stumbled upon a sight that would leave an indelible mark on my heart: a wedding ceremony.

There, against the backdrop of the setting sun and the gentle lapping of waves, two people were pledging their lives to each other. Venecia and I stood at a respectful distance, watching in awe as the couple exchanged vows. The love and joy radiating from them were palpable, their commitment to each other a testament to the resilience of the human spirit and the enduring power of love.

As I watched this beautiful moment unfold, I couldn't help but reflect on my own journey. 5 years ago, mired in the depths of addiction, the idea of standing on a beautiful beach, sober and in love, would have seemed like an impossible dream. Yet here I was, not only witnessing this beautiful union but also contemplating my own future with Venecia.

The wedding ceremony, so unexpectedly encountered, became a powerful metaphor for my recovery journey. Like a marriage, recovery requires daily commitment, unwavering dedication, and a willingness to face both joys and challenges together. It reminded me of the promises I had made to myself, to my higher power, and to my community in recovery.

That night, as Venecia and I sat on our hotel balcony, listening to the rhythmic sound of the waves, I shared with her the profound impact the day had had on me. We talked about our own relationship, our dreams for the future, and the gratitude we both felt for the path that had led us to this moment.

The next day, we embarked on an exploration of the local culture. The Dominican Republic, with its rich history and vibrant traditions, offered a stark reminder of the resilience that runs deep in the human spirit. As we visited local markets and interacted with the warm and welcoming Dominican people, I was struck by their joyful approach to life despite the economic challenges many of them faced.

This resilience resonated deeply with me, echoing the strength I had discovered within myself through the process of recovery. It reinforced a crucial lesson I had learned in AA and continued to embrace: that true happiness and fulfillment come not from external circumstances, but from internal peace and connection with others.

One afternoon, we visited a local cacao farm, where we learned about the process of chocolate making. As I watched the farmers carefully tending to the cacao trees and processing the beans, I was reminded of the patience and dedication required in recovery. Like the transformation of bitter cacao beans into sweet chocolate, recovery is a process of transformation that requires time, effort, and faith.

Throughout our stay in Punta Cana, I maintained my commitment to my spiritual practice. Each morning, I would wake early to meditate on the beach, the sound of the waves providing a soothing backdrop to my reflections. In these quiet moments, I found myself filled with gratitude - for my sobriety, for Venecia's love and support, and for the beauty that surrounded us.

As our trip drew to a close, Venecia and I spent our last evening once again walking along the beach. The memory of the wedding we had witnessed on our first night came flooding back, and in that moment, I felt a deep sense of peace and certainty about our future together.

Leaving Punta Cana, I carried with me not just memories of sun-soaked beaches and warm Caribbean hospitality, but profound insights about love, commitment, and resilience. The unexpected wedding we witnessed had become a powerful symbol of the journey I was on - a journey of recovery, of love, and of continual growth and transformation.

As we boarded the plane home, I reflected on how far I had come since my first sober trip to Cancun two years earlier. My recovery had deepened, my relationship with Venecia had blossomed, and my understanding of resilience had expanded. I was eager to see how these insights would integrate into my life back home and how they would shape the next legs of my journey.

Little did I know then that my path would eventually lead me to Narcotics Anonymous in 2020, opening up new avenues of growth and connection. But in that moment, as the coastline of Punta Cana receded beneath us, I felt profoundly grateful for the lessons learned and the love shared in this beautiful corner of the Caribbean.

The rhythms of resilience I had witnessed in Punta Cana - in the enduring love of a newly married couple, in the joyful spirit of the Dominican people, and in my own continuing journey of recovery - had become a part of me. They formed another layer in the tapestry of experiences that was shaping my spiritual journey across continents and through recovery.

As we flew home, I closed my eyes and offered a silent prayer of thanks - for the gift of sobriety, for the love I had found, and for the endless capacity for growth and renewal that I was discovering within myself and in the world around me. The journey was far from over, and I looked forward with hope and anticipation to the adventures and insights that lay ahead.

■ Chapter 3: Durban - Unity in Diversity and Labor Solidarity

As the plane touched down in Durban in 2023, I felt a surge of anticipation. This leg of my journey held special significance - I was here not just as a traveler, but as a delegate of the ILWU Local 10, participating in the 50th anniversary commemoration of the Durban Dock Workers strike in South Africa. The weight of this responsibility, coupled with the excitement of exploring a new continent, filled me with a mix of emotions.

Durban greeted me with a riot of colors, sounds, and smells. The city's vibrant energy was immediately apparent, from the bustling markets filled with traditional Zulu crafts to the modern skyscrapers lining the beachfront. But beneath the surface vitality, I could sense the complex history that had shaped this place - a history of struggle, resilience, and the ongoing journey towards reconciliation and equality.

My first week was spent at the University of Durban, where our delegation from San Francisco Local 10 International Longshore and Warehouse Union stood in solidarity with our South African counterparts. As I listened to the stories of the 1973 strike, I was struck by the parallels with our own struggles in the ILWU. The Black Durban dock workers, like us, had fought for fair wages, better working conditions, and dignity in their labor. Their strike had been a pivotal moment in the anti-apartheid struggle, demonstrating the power of organized labor to effect social change.

One speaker, an older man named Joseph Dube, South Africa Docks Transport Workers General Secretary who had participated in the '73 strike, spoke with passion about the unity they had found in their solidarity. "We were Zulu, Xhosa, Indian, Colored," he said, "but on the docks, we were one. Our strength was in our unity." His words resonated deeply with me, reminding me of the importance of solidarity across all divides in our union work.

Throughout my stay in Durban, I was continually struck by the way in which diversity was not just tolerated, but celebrated. In the markets of Warwick Junction, I saw Muslim, Hindu, and Christian traders working side by side. In the city of uMhlanga, I witnessed a blend of traditional Zulu culture with modern urban life. This coexistence of different cultures, religions, and traditions was a powerful testament to the possibility of unity in diversity.

One of the most profound experiences of my time in Durban came during a visit to a local community center in KwaMashu township. Here, I met a group of young activists who were working to address issues of poverty, education, and health in their community. Their energy and commitment reminded me of my own early days in the union, but what struck me most was their embrace of the concept of Ubuntu.

"Ubuntu," one woman named Nise, the director of the Bat Centre of Art in Durban, explained to me, "means 'I am because we are.' It's the idea that our humanity is interconnected. We can only truly thrive when we recognize and nurture our connections to others." This philosophy, so deeply ingrained in African culture, offered a powerful counterpoint to the individualism often celebrated in Western societies.

As I reflected on Ubuntu, I realized how closely it aligned with the principles of solidarity that had guided my work in the labor movement. Wasn't this the very essence of what we strived for in our unions - the recognition that our individual well-being is inextricably linked to the well-being of our fellow workers and our broader community?

While I didn't attend any AA or NA meetings during my time in South Africa, I was grateful to be traveling with two union brothers who were also living sober. Their presence and our shared commitment to recovery provided a sense of continuity and support, even as we immersed ourselves in new experiences and cultures.

One of the most spiritually significant moments of my trip came early one morning at the uMhlanga Lighthouse. I had risen before dawn, drawn by an inexplicable urge to witness the sunrise over the Indian Ocean. As I stood there, watching the sky slowly transform from inky black to a palette of pinks and golds, I felt an overwhelming sense of gratitude and connection.

In that moment, as the first rays of sunlight kissed the waves, I found myself moved to prayer. I thanked my higher power for my continued sobriety, for the opportunity to be in this beautiful place, and for the strength and resilience I had witnessed in the people I had met. The vastness of the ocean before me seemed to mirror the endless possibilities of recovery and growth.

As I prayed, I reflected on my journey - not just the physical journey that had brought me to this lighthouse in South Africa, but the spiritual journey of my recovery. From my first sober trip to Cancun in 2014, through the lessons learned in Punta Cana, to this moment in Durban, I could see how each experience had built upon the last, deepening my understanding of myself and my place in the world.

The light from the lighthouse, steadfast and unwavering, reminded me of the guiding principles of my recovery program. Just as this beacon helped ships navigate treacherous waters, the 12 steps had been my guide through the challenges of life. And just as the lighthouse stood strong against the elements, so too had my recovery weathered the storms of life.

As my time in Durban drew to a close, I found myself filled with a renewed sense of purpose. The spirit of Ubuntu, the solidarity I had witnessed among the dock workers, and the resilience of the South African people in the face of historical injustices - all of these had left an indelible mark on my heart.

Leaving Durban, I carried with me not just memories of a vibrant city and warm hospitality, but profound insights about unity, diversity, and the power of collective action. The journey had reinforced my commitment to both my recovery and my work in the labor movement, showing me how deeply intertwined these two paths were.

As the coastline of South Africa receded beneath the plane, I closed my eyes and offered a silent prayer of gratitude. For the lessons learned, the connections made, and the continued gift of sobriety that allowed me to experience it all with clarity and presence.

Little did I know then that my next destination, Honolulu, would bring new challenges and opportunities for growth. But in that moment, as I flew towards home, I felt profoundly grateful for the journey so far and excited for what lay ahead. The spirit of Ubuntu, the unwavering light of the uMhlanga Lighthouse, and the rhythms of resilience I had witnessed in Durban had become a part of me, guiding me forward on my continued journey of recovery and discovery.

■ Chapter 4: Honolulu - Aloha Spirit and Recovery Brotherhood

As the plane descended towards Honolulu in 2024, the vast expanse of the Pacific Ocean gave way to the lush, green mountains of Oahu. The sight of Diamond Head crater and the gleaming skyline of Waikiki filled me with a sense of anticipation. This final leg of my journey promised to bring together threads from my previous experiences, weaving them into a fabric of spiritual understanding and personal growth.

But this trip was different from the others. I wasn't alone this time. Accompanying me were my recovery brothers: Rajala Scott, Joey Harrison, and Aaron. Our shared journey in recovery had brought us together for this adventure, adding a new dimension to my ongoing spiritual odyssey.

Our first morning in Honolulu, we found ourselves drawn to the beach. As we walked along the shore, the soft sand beneath our feet and the gentle lapping of waves created a soothing rhythm. It was a stark contrast to the bustling docks of San Francisco, yet I felt a familiar connection to the water, a reminder of the vast interconnectedness of our world.

As we stood there, taking in the beauty of our surroundings, I was moved to suggest a prayer. Together, we formed a circle on the beach, our hands joined in unity. We prayed for safety on our journey, expressed gratitude for our continued sobriety, and asked for the wisdom to fully appreciate the experiences that lay ahead. This moment of shared spirituality set the tone for our entire trip, reminding us of the strong bonds formed in recovery.

Later that day, we made our way to the boat pier, where we were scheduled to take a submarine tour. Before boarding, we once again joined hands in prayer. The act of praying with my recovery brothers in this new setting - with the vast ocean before us and the unknown depths below - was profoundly moving. We thanked our higher power for the gift of sobriety that allowed us to be present for such experiences, and we asked for protection as we embarked on our underwater adventure.

The submarine tour itself was a metaphor for our recovery journey. As we descended into the depths, leaving the familiar world behind, I couldn't help but think of the courage it takes to dive into the unknown waters of sobriety. The colorful fish and coral reefs we saw reminded me of the beauty and richness of life that recovery has allowed me to experience.

One of the highlights of our trip was attending the "Nooners" 12-step meeting in Honolulu. Sitting in a circle with locals and fellow travelers, I was struck once again by the universal language of recovery. Despite our diverse backgrounds, we shared a common bond, a shared understanding of the struggles and triumphs of living sober.

As I shared my story with the group, touching on my journey from Cancun to Punta Cana, from Durban to Honolulu, I felt a deep sense of gratitude. Each of these destinations had contributed to my spiritual growth, and now, here in Hawaii, I was able to give back by sharing my experience, strength, and hope with others.

The Aloha spirit, which permeates every aspect of Hawaiian culture, resonated deeply with the principles of our recovery program. The concept of treating others with love and respect, of living in harmony with the world around us, aligned perfectly with the spiritual awakening I had experienced through working the 12 steps.

During our stay, we took time to explore the island's natural beauty. We hiked through lush rainforests, swam in crystal-clear waters, and watched the sun set over volcanic landscapes. Each of these experiences reinforced the Hawaiian view of nature as a living, breathing entity deserving of respect and reverence.

One day, we visited a few local farms where we learned about current Hawaiian agriculture. As we drank the fresh coffee, took photos of pineapples, and ate macadamia nuts, I was reminded of the importance of giving back, of nurturing not just our own recovery but the recovery of others. The tour guide spoke of their connection to the land with a reverence that echoed the spiritual connection I felt to my recovery journey.

We also indulged in the local cuisine, savoring the sweetness of fresh bananas and the rich flavor of macadamia nuts. These simple pleasures were a reminder of the joys of sober living, of being present and grateful for each moment and experience.

As our time in Honolulu drew to a close, I found myself reflecting on the journey that had brought me here. From my first sober trip to Cancun a decade ago, through the lessons learned in Punta Cana and Durban, to this moment in Hawaii with my recovery brothers, I could see how each experience had built upon the last, deepening my understanding of myself and my place in the world.

On our last evening, we gathered on Waikiki Beach to watch the sunset. As the sky transformed into a canvas of vibrant colors, I felt an overwhelming sense of gratitude. Gratitude for my sobriety, for the fellowship of my recovery brothers, and for the journey that had brought me to this moment.

As the last light faded from the sky and the first stars began to appear, I made a silent promise to myself. I would carry the lessons of this journey with me - the wisdom of ancient civilizations, the resilience of peoples who had overcome great adversity, the power of unity in diversity, and the importance of living in harmony with the natural world. These insights would continue to inform not just my personal recovery, but my work with the union and my engagement with my community back home.

With the gentle lapping of waves as a backdrop, we closed our eyes and offered a final prayer of thanks - to the lands that had welcomed us, to the people who had shared their wisdom, and to the higher power that had guided us on this remarkable journey. As we prepared to return home, I knew that while our physical travels were coming to an end, our spiritual journey was far from over.

The Aloha spirit, the fellowship of recovery, and the natural beauty of Hawaii had become part of our shared experience, another thread in the tapestry of our ongoing recovery. As we boarded the plane home, I felt a renewed commitment to carrying this spirit of Aloha, this sense of interconnectedness and love, into every aspect of my life.

The journey across four continents had come full circle, each destination offering its own unique lessons and insights. And yet, as we lifted off from Honolulu, I knew that in many ways, the most important journey - the daily walk of recovery - was one that would continue long after we returned home.

■ Epilogue: The Journey Continues

As the plane touched down in San Francisco, I felt a strange mix of emotions. There was joy at returning home, excitement to share my experiences with friends and colleagues, but also a tinge of nostalgia for the remarkable journey that had come to an end. Yet, as I collected my luggage and made my way through the familiar corridors of SFO, I realized that in many ways, the journey was far from over.

The experiences of the past decade had transformed me in ways I was only beginning to understand. The ancient wisdom of Chichén Itzá, the resilient spirit of Punta Cana, the unity in diversity of Durban, and the Aloha spirit of Honolulu - all of these had become part of me, reshaping my perspective and deepening my understanding of the world and my place in it.

As I stood on the deck of my San Francisco home that evening, gazing out at the familiar sight of the Golden Gate Bridge, I reflected on how far I had come. Ten years ago, when I first embarked on this journey with my trip to Cancun, I was three years into my recovery with Alcoholics Anonymous. Now, after thirteen years of continuous sobriety, including my transition to Narcotics Anonymous in 2020, I stood here a changed man.

Each destination had offered its own unique lessons, contributing to my spiritual growth and recovery:

In Cancun and Chichén Itzá, I learned about the importance of connecting with something greater than myself. The ancient Mayan ruins reminded me that, like their enduring structures, recovery requires a strong foundation and daily maintenance.

Punta Cana taught me about resilience and the power of love. Witnessing a wedding on the beach with Venecia reinforced the parallels between the commitments we make in recovery and the commitments we make to our loved ones.

Durban showed me the strength that comes from unity in diversity. The concept of Ubuntu - "I am because we are" - deepened my understanding of the interconnectedness we share in recovery and in the labor movement.

And finally, Honolulu, with its Aloha spirit, brought everything full circle. Traveling with my recovery brothers and attending meetings there reminded me of the universal language of recovery and the importance of fellowship.

Throughout these journeys, the act of praying in each location took on special significance. Whether it was on the beach in Cancun, at the uMhlanga Lighthouse in Durban, or with my recovery brothers on the boat pier in Honolulu, each prayer was a moment of connection - with my higher power, with the beauty of my surroundings, and with my innermost self.

The spiritual awakenings I experienced as a result of working the 12 steps year after year were amplified by these travels. Each new chip I received, marking another year of sobriety, was not just a personal achievement but a reminder of the global community of recovery I had become a part of.

As I looked out over the Bay, my mind drifted to the words of T.S. Eliot:

"We shall not cease from exploration
And the end of all our exploring
Will be to arrive where we started
And know the place for the first time."

These words resonated deeply with me now. I had traveled thousands of miles, only to return home and see it with new eyes. The journey had come full circle, yet it was also just beginning.

I knew that the insights and experiences gained on my travels would continue to unfold in the months and years to come. They would inform my work with the ILWU, enrich my relationships, and deepen my spiritual life. The journey of discovery, I realized, was not a finite thing with a clear beginning and end, but a continuous process of growth, learning, and transformation.

As the sun set over the Bay, painting the sky in hues reminiscent of the sunsets I had witnessed in Cancun, Punta Cana, Durban, and Honolulu, I felt a profound sense of gratitude. Gratitude for the opportunity to undertake this journey, for the people I had met along the way, for the wisdom shared and the lessons learned.

But more than that, I felt grateful for the journey that lay ahead - the continued exploration of self, community, and spirit that would shape the rest of my life. For I had learned that every place holds the potential for revelation, every person we meet can be a teacher, and every experience, if approached with an open heart and mind, can lead us closer to understanding our place in the vast, interconnected fabric of life.

As darkness fell and the lights of the city began to twinkle, I made a silent vow. I would honor the gifts of my journey by living each day with the same spirit of curiosity, openness, and reverence that had guided me through Chichén Itzá, Punta Cana, Durban, and Honolulu. For in doing so, I knew that the sacred journey would continue, unfolding day by day, revealing new wonders and insights in even the most familiar of surroundings.

With a heart full of hope and a spirit renewed, I turned from the view and stepped back into my home. The physical journey had ended, but the spiritual voyage - the ongoing process of recovery, of getting through challenges to reach new understandings - was just beginning. And I was ready, eager to see where it would lead me next, one day at a time.

■ Acknowledgments

As I reflect on the journey that led to this book, I am overwhelmed with gratitude for the many people who have supported me, inspired me, and walked alongside me on this path of recovery and discovery.

First and foremost, I want to thank my Higher Power, whose grace and guidance have been the bedrock of my recovery and the source of strength for this incredible journey across four continents.

To my former fiancée, Venecia Margarita, your love, patience, and unwavering support have been my anchor through every step of this journey. Thank you for sharing the beauty of Punta Cana with me and for being a constant reminder of the power of love and commitment.

I am deeply grateful to my recovery brothers - Rajala Scott, Joey Harrison, and Aaron. Your friendship and the shared experience of our trip to Honolulu have enriched my life and my recovery in ways I never imagined possible. Thank you for your strength, your laughter, and your fellowship.

To my first love in recovery Regina Haugebook, thank you for accompanying me to that pivotal Catholic Mass and exploring the awesome wonders of Cancun in 2014. Your presence at the beginning of this journey was more significant than you may have realized.

I owe a debt of gratitude to my brothers and sisters in the ILWU Local 10. Your solidarity and commitment to justice have been a constant source of inspiration. Special thanks to those who stood with me in Durban, commemorating the 50th anniversary of the dock worker strike. Your dedication to our shared cause reminds me daily of the power of unity and collective action.

To the countless individuals I met on my travels - from the vibrant streets of Cancun to the beaches of Punta Cana, from the townships of Durban to the shores of Honolulu - thank you for sharing your stories, your wisdom, and your resilience with me. You have expanded my understanding of the world and deepened my faith in the human spirit.

I am profoundly grateful to the fellowships of Alcoholics Anonymous and Narcotics Anonymous. The rooms of recovery have been my school, my sanctuary, and my home. To everyone who has shared their experience, strength, and hope with me over these 13 years of recovery - thank you. Your stories have lit my path and your support has lifted me up countless times.

To my sponsor Laron S., whose full name remains anonymous in keeping with our traditions, thank you for your guidance, your tough love, and your unwavering belief in me. Your example has shown me what it means to live the principles of our program in all my affairs.

A special thank you to my mom, Barbara Scott, whose keen eye and insightful feedback helped shape most of my books into their final form. Your expertise and patience has been invaluable.

To Bysscott.org and my entire publishing team, thank you for believing in this project and for your hard work in bringing it to fruition.

Finally, to my family - both blood and chosen - your love and support have been the wind beneath my wings. Thank you for standing by me through the darkest times and for celebrating every milestone of my recovery journey.

This book, and the journey it chronicles, would not have been possible without each and every one of you. From the bottom of my heart, thank you.

■ About the Author

I am a longshore worker, a union activist, and a person in long-term recovery. My journey has taken me from the depths of addiction to the shores of four continents, each step bringing new insights, challenges, and opportunities for growth.

For over two decades, I have been a proud member of the International Longshore and Warehouse Union (ILWU) Local 10 in San Francisco. My work on the docks has taught me the value of hard work, solidarity, and standing up for what's right. It's also given me a global perspective on labor issues and human rights, leading me to participate in international events like the 50th anniversary commemoration of the Durban Dock Workers strike in South Africa.

But my life hasn't always been defined by union activism and global travels. For many years, I struggled with addiction, a battle that nearly cost me everything. In 2011, I found my way into the rooms of Alcoholics Anonymous, marking the beginning of a transformative journey in recovery.

For the first nine years of my sobriety, AA was my lifeline. The fellowship, the 12 steps, and the spiritual principles of the program helped me rebuild my life one day at a time. In 2020, I transitioned to Narcotics Anonymous, finding a new home and new perspectives in this fellowship.

My recovery journey has been intertwined with my travels. From my first sober trip to Cancun in 2014 to my most recent adventure in Honolulu with my recovery brothers, each destination has deepened my spiritual understanding and strengthened my commitment to living a life of purpose and service.

Today, I am grateful to celebrate over 13 years of continuous sobriety. This journey has taught me that recovery is not just about abstinence from substances, but about spiritual growth, connection with others, and finding meaning in life's experiences.

When I'm not working on the docks or attending recovery meetings, you can find me exploring the natural beauty of the San Francisco Bay Area, often with a beautiful woman, by my side. I'm an avid reader, always eager to learn from the wisdom of others, whether it's in ancient Mayan ruins or modern self-help books.

Writing this book has been a labor of love, a way to share the lessons I've learned and the hope I've found on my journey across continents and through recovery. My greatest hope is that by sharing my experience, strength, and hope, I can inspire others to embark on their own journeys of discovery and healing.

Remember, no matter where you are in your journey, you are never alone. There is always hope, always a new day, always a chance to begin again.

■ Glossary

12 Steps: A set of guiding principles outlining a course of action for recovery from addiction, compulsion, or other behavioral problems.

AA (Alcoholics Anonymous): An international fellowship of men and women who have had a drinking problem. It is nonprofessional, self-supporting, multiracial, apolitical, and available almost everywhere.

Aloha Spirit: A Hawaiian concept of treating others with love, respect, and kindness, embodying the warmth and sincerity of Hawaiian hospitality.

Chichén Itzá: An ancient Mayan city located in Mexico's Yucatán Peninsula, known for its stepped pyramids and astronomical significance.

Kukulkan: Also known as the Temple of Kukulcán (pyramid of El Castillo), it is the central pyramid of Chichén Itzá, notable for its astronomical alignments.

Higher Power: A term used in 12-step programs to refer to a power greater than oneself, which can be interpreted according to individual belief.

Ho'oponopono: A Hawaiian practice of reconciliation and forgiveness.

ILWU (International Longshore and Warehouse Union): A labor union primarily representing dock workers on the West Coast of the United States, Hawaii, and Alaska.

NA (Narcotics Anonymous): A nonprofit fellowship or society of men and women for whom drugs had become a major problem. It follows a 12-step model adapted from Alcoholics Anonymous.

Nooners Meeting: A common term for 12-step meetings held during lunch hour, typically at noon.

Pono: A Hawaiian concept of righteousness, balance, and harmony with the natural world.

Recovery: The process of change through which individuals improve their health and wellness, live self-directed lives, and strive to reach their full potential, particularly in the context of overcoming addiction.

Resilience: The capacity to recover quickly from difficulties; toughness.

Sacred Cenote: A natural sinkhole at Chichén Itzá, believed by the ancient Maya to be a gateway to the underworld.

Sobriety: The state of not being intoxicated; in recovery contexts, it often refers to abstinence from alcohol and drugs.

Solidarity: Unity or agreement of feeling or action, especially among individuals with a common interest; mutual support within a group.

Sponsor: In 12-step programs, an individual with significant clean time who guides a newer member through the steps and offers support in recovery.

Macadamia (Hawaiian nuts): Macadamia nuts, originally from Australia, were first cultivated in Hawaii around 1881.

Ubuntu: An African philosophy meaning "I am because we are," emphasizing the interconnectedness of human beings.

uMhlanga Lighthouse: A lighthouse located in uMhlanga, north of Durban, South Africa, known for its distinctive red and white color scheme.

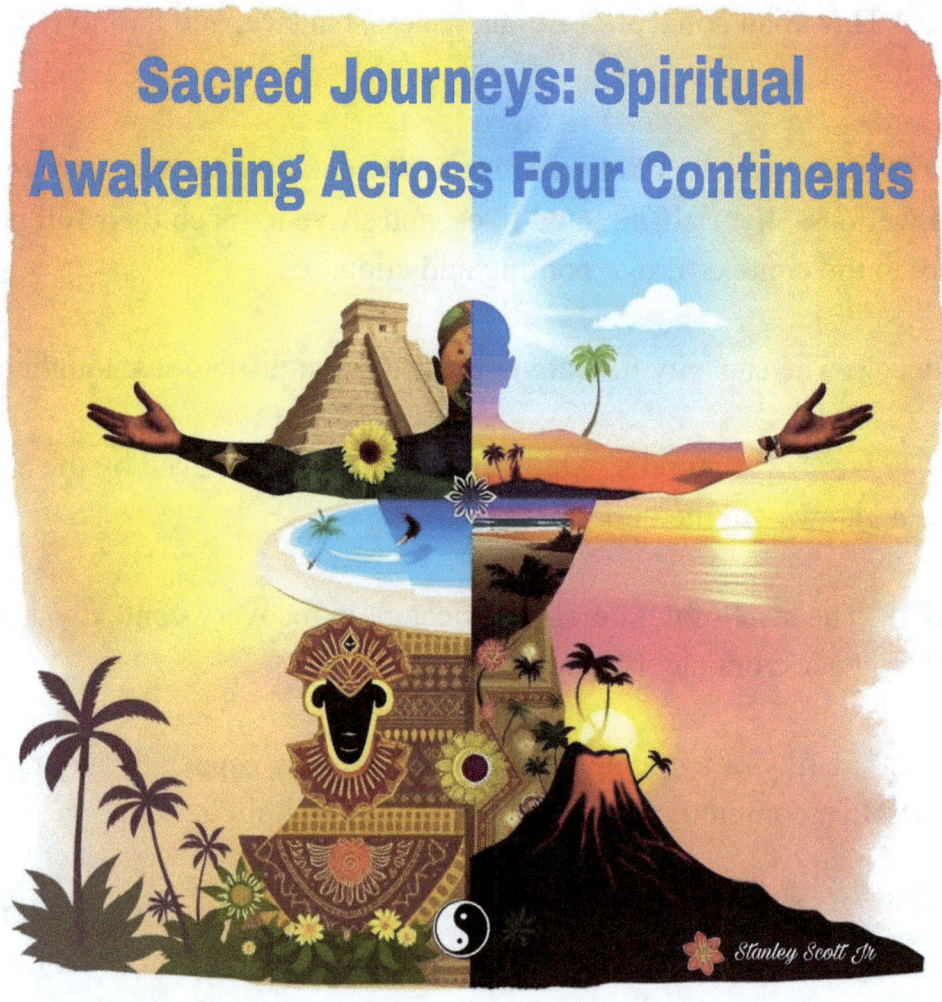

Sacred Journeys: Spiritual Awakening Across Four Continents

■ Images of my Sacred Journeys Across Four Continents:

☆ Chichén Itzá, Yucatan Peninsula

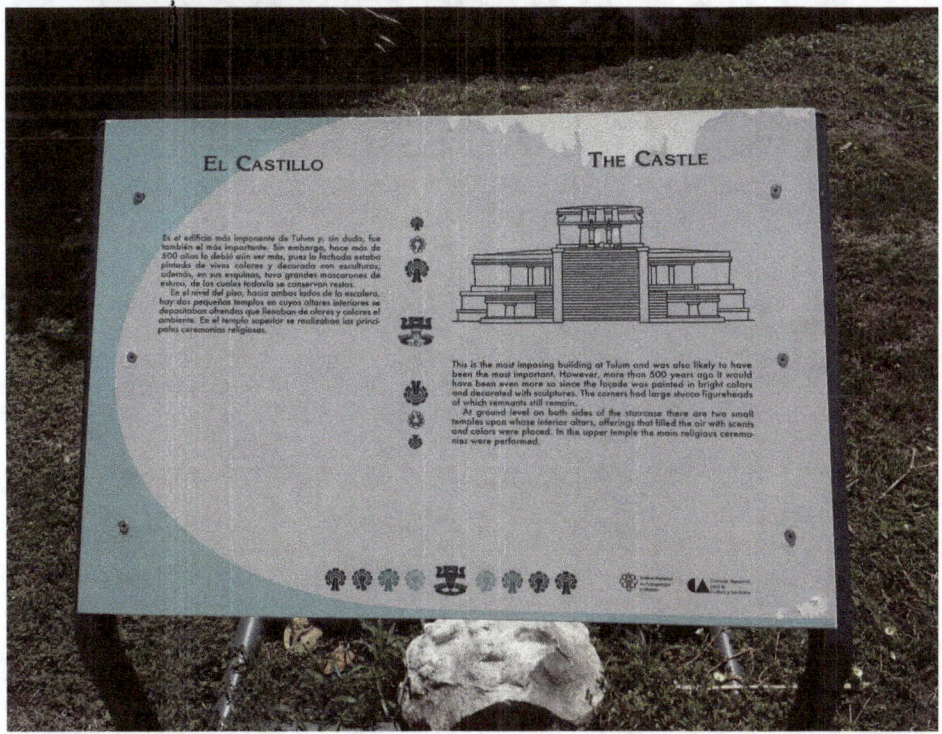

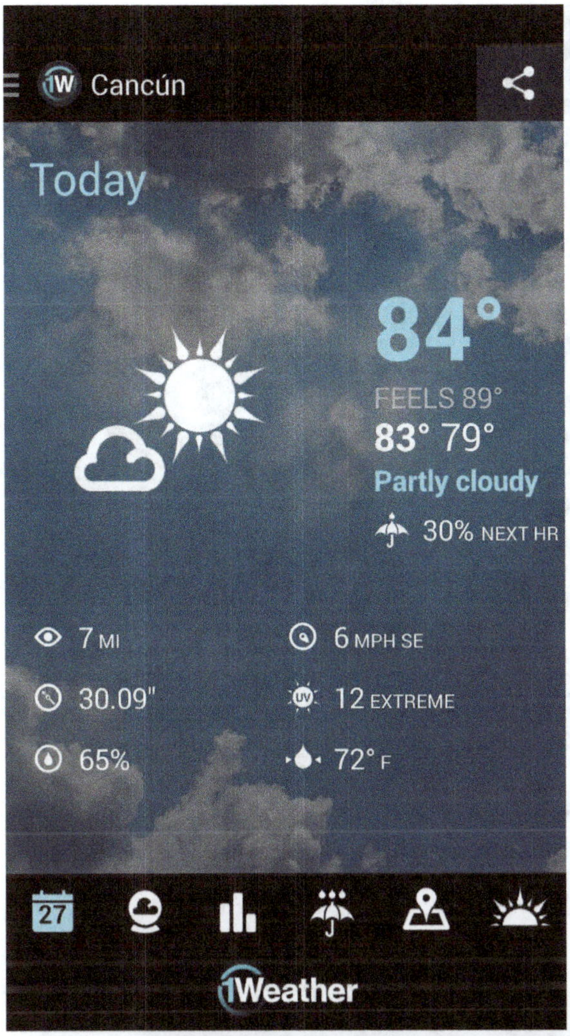
Cancún
Today
84°
FEELS 89°
83° 79°
Partly cloudy
30% NEXT HR
7 MI
6 MPH SE
30.09"
12 EXTREME
65%
72° F
27
1Weather

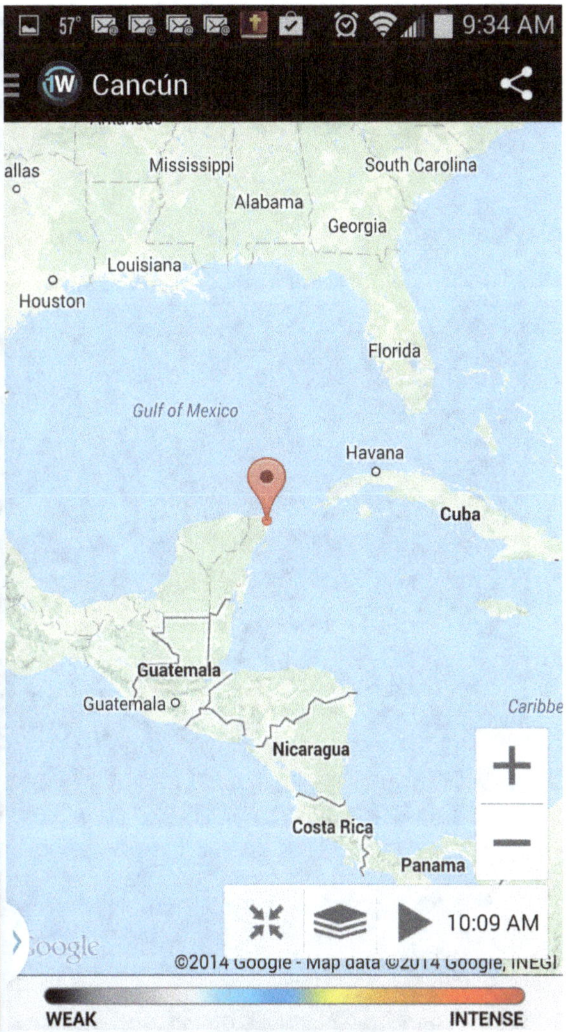
57°
9:34 AM
Cancún
Mississippi
South Carolina
Alabama
Georgia
Louisiana
Houston
Florida
Gulf of Mexico
Havana
Cuba
Guatemala
Guatemala
Nicaragua
Costa Rica
Panama
10:09 AM
©2014 Google - Map data ©2014 Google, INEGI
WEAK
INTENSE

CANCUN

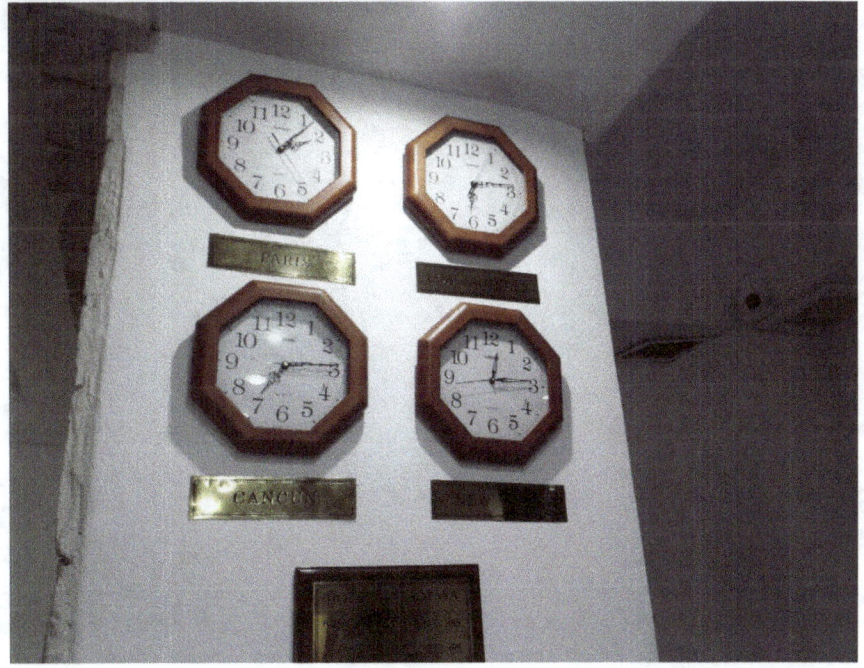

45

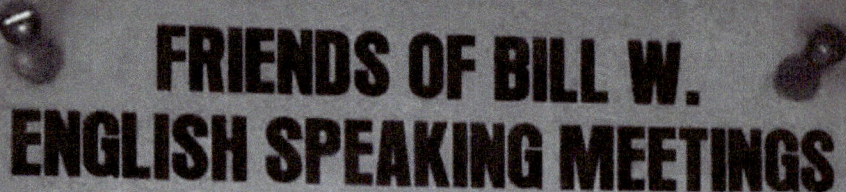

FRIENDS OF BILL W.
ENGLISH SPEAKING MEETINGS

UNIDAD SERVICIO

AA

RECUPERACION

DAILY 6:15 TO 7:15 P.M.

I am responsible...

When anyone, anywhere,
reaches out for help, I want
the hand of A.A. always to be there.
And for that: I am responsible.

☆ Punta Cana, Dominican Republic

☆ Durban, South Africa

ILWU South African Delegates
By S.Scott

Durban University of Technology is among the 10 universities featured in U-Multirank for South Africa.

This large public university, situated in Durban, has an enrollment of 34,279 students according to data from 2019 or the latest available information.

The university was established in 2002.

Dawn in Durban
By S Scott

A Durban Morning
By S Scott

Lighthouse RD. Durban
By S Scott

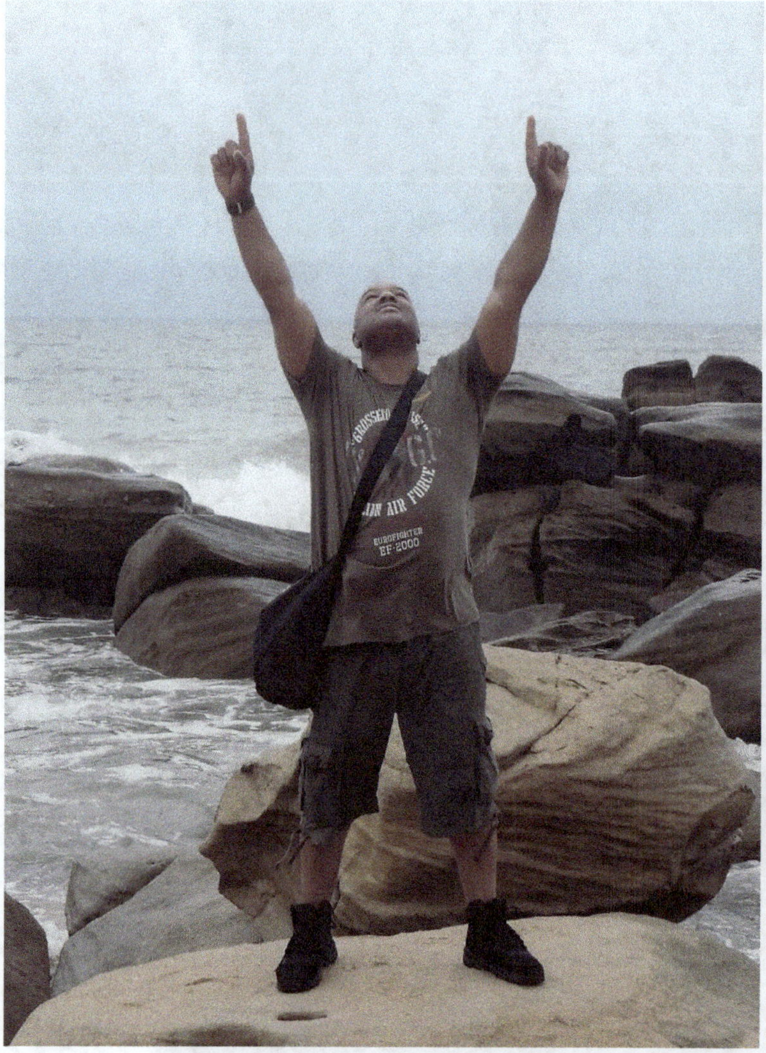

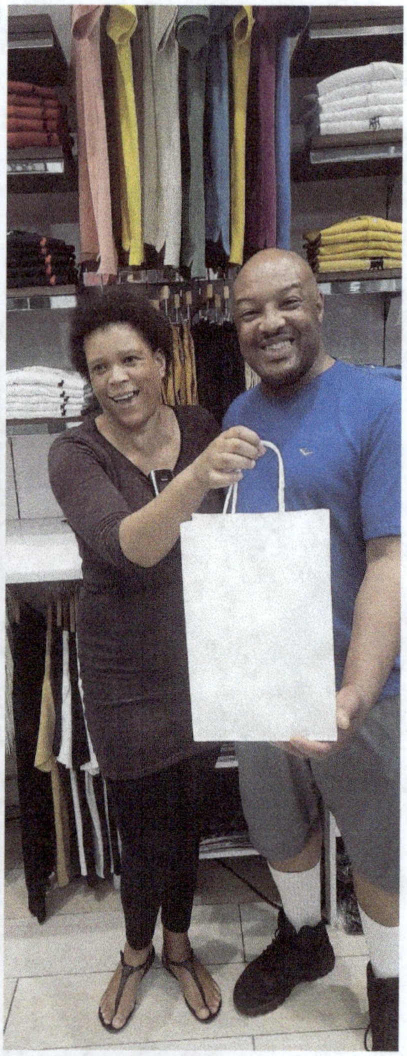

drip
LOUNGE SA
Arabella

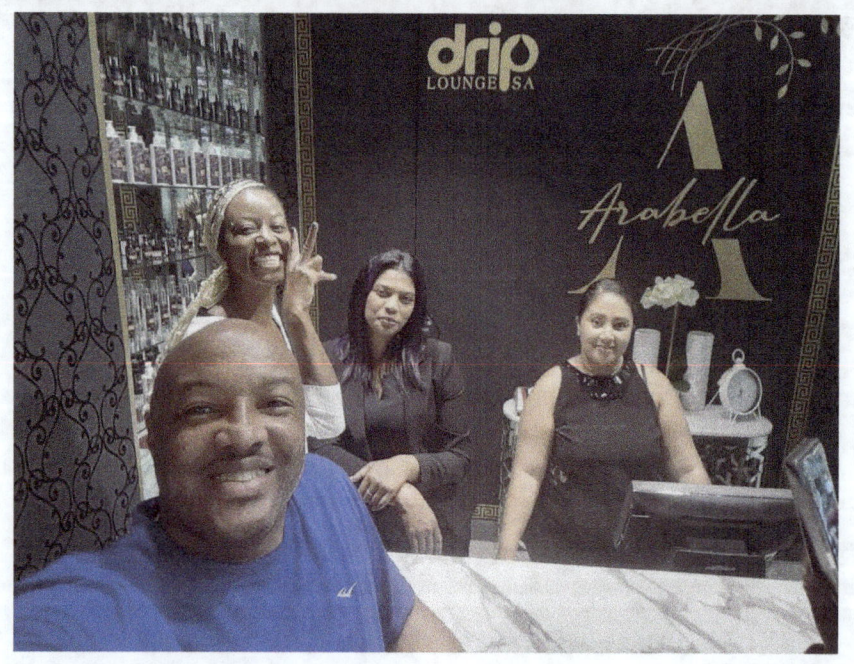

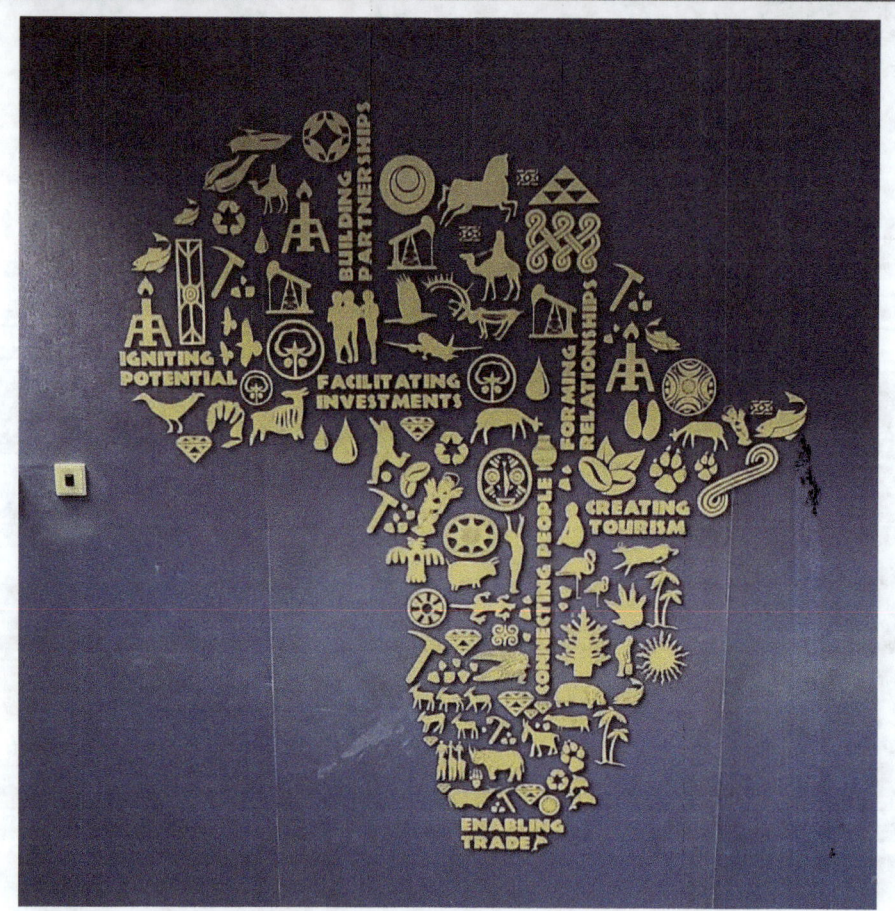

☆ Soweto, South Africa

Local 10 delegation marks 50th anniversary of the Durban Strikes

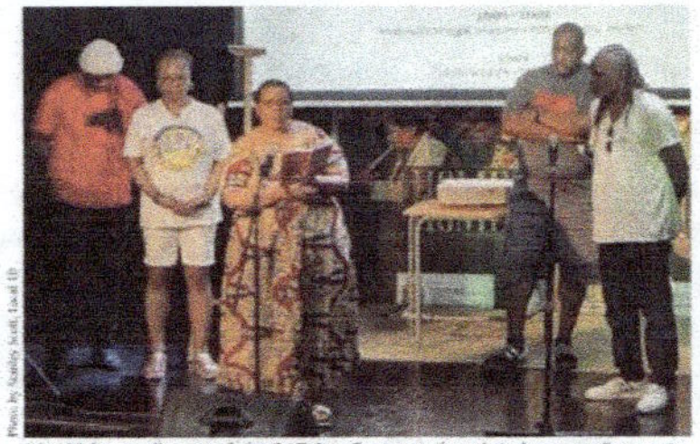

Nise Malanga, director of the BAT Arts Centre at the microphone reading poetry from her book addressing the struggle of Black workers. Local 10 members on stage from left to right are David Newton, Vanetta Hamlin, Ed Henderson, and Andre Dawkins.

continued from page 1

Archie Brown were among those active in those years. These rank-and-file driven work stoppages were unprecedented in the United States, though workers in some other countries also engaged in similar actions in solidarity with the struggle against apartheid. In 1990, Nelson and his then-wife, Winnie Mandela, visited Oakland, the last stop on their first tour of the U.S. At a packed Oakland Coliseum, Mandela devoted the first ten percent of his speech to thanking ILWU Local 10 for standing down in solidarity with Black workers in South Africa.

Because of Local 10's longstanding solidarity with the struggle of Black workers in South Africa, it's not entirely surprising that Local 10's Executive Board voted to send a delegation to South Africa to remember the historic Durban Strikes. The weeklong trip was a tremendous opportunity to engage with dockers, other unionists, and activists in South Africa, among the important countries in Africa and the Southern Hemisphere. Ultimately, 14 current members and pensioners made the trip, part of a long tradition of sending rank-and-file members to attend conferences and visit dockworkers across the world.

South Africa's long legacy of white supremacy

Before 1994, South Africa was notorious for being among the most racist and oppressive countries on earth. For centuries, going back to the 1650s, a white minority — composed mostly of Afrikaners (people of Dutch descent) and Anglos — ruthlessly exploited the large majority of the people who come from many different African ethnic groups (Zulus, Xhosas, Sothos, and more) as well as Asian Indians and so-called "Coloured" people (a separate legal category for mixed race people).

The fight for freedom

As far back as the 1910s, Africans, Indians, and Coloureds worked separately and together to overturn the brutal white supremacist regime. Shortly after WWII, the government formally instituted apartheid — doubling down on racism and fascism just three years after the defeat of the Nazis. The anti-apartheid movement spent decades trying to peacefully gain equal rights before adopting "armed struggle" in the early 1960s. By then, Nelson Mandela was a leader in the largest and best-known anti-apartheid organization, the African National Congress (ANC).

Sharpeville Massacre

Starting in 1960 with the Sharpeville Massacre, when about 70 peaceful Black protesters were killed by the police, and continuing for the next four years, nearly all domestic opposition was wiped out due to ferocious government repression. Activists were imprisoned, killed, politically banned, driven underground and into exile, or otherwise silenced. The ANC and Pan-African Congress were banned, and the Communist Party already had been. Mandela went underground for several years but, ultimately was captured and, in 1964, along with other leaders, was sentenced to life in prison on the barren Robben Island, six miles off Cape Town on the Atlantic Coast. He would not be seen in public for decades.

Durban Strikes

After nearly a so-called "quiet decade" in the struggle against apartheid, the Durban Strikes erupted in January 1973. These strikes involved upwards of 100,000 Black and Asian workers from more than 150 companies. This uprising shocked the nation and reignited the anti-apartheid movement that mostly had been quiescent due to earlier repression. Importantly, though not widely known, dockworkers in Durban, then and still at the heart of the economy, had primed the pump by striking in 1969 and, again, in late 1972. In other words, by shutting the harbor for days, dockers "set the table" for the Durban Strikes. While it would take another twenty years of intense struggle, inside South Africa and globally, apartheid ultimately was beaten.

Commemorating the 50th anniversary

While those who know South African history appreciate the Durban Strikes' significance, the average South African on the street doesn't. So, the commemoration of the 50th anniversary of the Durban Strikes was not exactly a huge event, at least as measured in numbers. But those who came together to remember this history and, at times celebrate it, included some of the foremost scholars and activists of labor and political economy in South Africa. In addition to discussing the anti-apartheid struggle of the 1970s and '80s, participants also discussed the ways this history might help us understand the troubling times of 2023 to chart a better future.

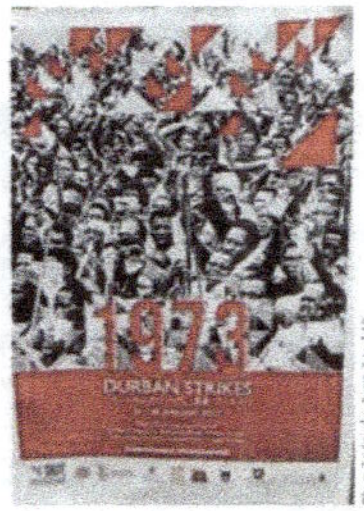

Current crisis

Despite its incredible, inspirational history of struggle to achieve multiracial democracy, South Africa faces serious problems. The ANC has lost its way, many of its leaders widely seen as corrupt, a once-great liberation party gone astray. Unemployment is rampant, and half the population lives in poverty. The country suffers from high crime, and climate change already is causing great problems. Economic inequality is rampant and deeply racialized. Electricity is shut down for hours a day, called "load shedding," which disrupts people's lives and the economy. Add Covid-19 and 350 years of racist colonialism, and it shouldn't come as a surprise that South African workers are struggling.

Scholars and activists converge

Local 10's delegation joined two conferences in Durban over the course of four very full days. The first was sponsored by South Africa History Online and hosted by the Durban University of Technology. Dozens of scholars and activists — many from the trade union movement and involved in the struggle since the 1970s — participated. Some people discussed their roles in the heady times of the 1970s, when the state regularly murdered activists and even assassinated activists in exile in Mozambique, Zimbabwe, and England. Some presented their research on labor, race relations, poverty, and politics. One night, the conference hosted an incredible musical performance by the 10-member Insurrection Ensemble, who performed the history and legacy of the Durban Strikes through the stories of a handful of women who struck a textile factory in 1973.

There also was a second, parallel conference organized to remember 1973 and reflect on how it could reenergize the labor movement, locally and globally, in 2023. This conference was cosponsored by the Revolutionary Trade Union of South Africa (RETUSA), a breakaway union from the South African Transport & Allied Workers Union (SATAWU), which represented nearly all dockers and other logistics workers across the country until the split, which mirrored other fissures in the South African labor movement. Joseph V. "JV" Dube previously led Durban's dockers in SATAWU before leading them into RETUSA. Hosted in the old harbor neighborhood at the BAT Centre, an important community and cultural arts space, this conference's main organizer was Dave Hemson, who was an important dock union organizer in the 1970s. Hemson, a white university student in the late 1960s, developed close relationships with the all-Black dock workforce—much like Harry Bridges did during the Big Strike of 1934.

On the first morning of this second conference, Hemson led a wonderful historic bus tour of The Point, the old waterfront neighborhood where many thousands of Zulu and Pondo dockers had once lived in nearby company-owned housing and loaded and unloaded ships in Africa's busiest port. When containers arrived in the late 1970s, the port "moved" to another part of the harbor, leaving The Point — right by the Ocean and near downtown — as prime for wiping out the old working-class area in favor of wealthier, and whiter residents. Sadly, the (old) Point has been entirely gentrified, much like is at risk in Oakland, where a scheme to enrich the A's sports franchise risks wiping out part of the Port.

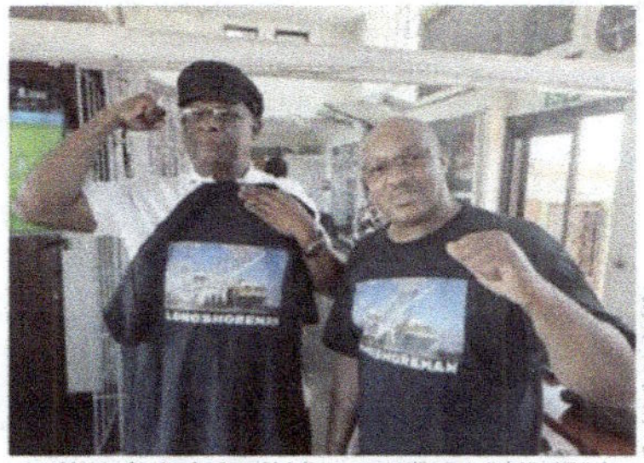

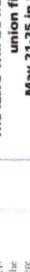

Local 10 member Stanley Scott (right) presents a t-shirt to Joseph V. "JV" Dube, General Secretary of RETUSA.

Legacy of solidarity

One of the other parallels between the ILWU and Durban dockers was that both have demonstrated a willingness to stop work in solidarity with liberation struggles in other countries. On April 21, 2008, the Chinese ship An Yue Jiang docked in Durban, carrying millions of rounds of ammunition for AK-47s, mortars, and rocket-propelled grenades. Zimbabwe's then-president, Robert Mugabe, purchased this arsenal to retain power amidst a highly contested election while his military and police beat thousands and killed hundreds of Zimbabweans. Mugabe's forces also brutally assaulted his rival, who had won the election's first round and served as Secretary-General of the Zimbabwe Congress of Trade Unions. Instead of unloading those weapons, the Durban branch of SATAWU embargoed the ship in solidarity with Zimbabwean workers. Subsequently, dockers in other southern African ports joined this boycott and the ship returned to China with its deadly cargo.

This action was not the first time that Durban dockers used their position at a choke point in support of social justice in another nation, and it echoed the ILWU's earlier efforts in the long struggle against apartheid, including the refusal of Local 10 and 34 members to touch South African cargo for 10 days in 1984. ILWU members also refused to load cargo for imperial Japan after it invaded China in the late 1930s.

These and other parallels forged deep connections between ILWU members and the dockers they met in Durban. Both sides very much were mindful of the need to build international networks that strengthen unionists and all workers. It should come as no surprise that, like the ILWU, the motto of most unions in South Africa is "An injury to one is an injury to all."

"The more that we can connect and build relationships with other workers around the world, the stronger we will be," said Local 10's Ed Henderson. "It's one thing to read about what's happening, and another thing to see it for yourself. Delegations like this help to build international camaraderie."

"The Durban trip was educational," said Local 10 member Stanley Scott. "We learned about the 1973 strike from researchers, and the cultural aspects of the strike from poets, singers, and musicians at the BAT Centre." When we got to the Port of Durban and saw all of the ships, I understood that we are the same dockworkers that unload these ships all over the world. That made me proud to be a longshoreman. We change the world every day."

Peter Cole is a professor of history at Western Illinois University and a research associate in the Society, Work, and Development Institute, University of the Witwatersrand in South Africa. His books include Dockworker Power: Race and Activism in Durban and the San Francisco Bay Area and Ben Fletcher: The Life & Times of a Black Wobbly.

ILWU to Hold Secretary-Treasurers Conference

The ILWU will be holding a conference for local union financial officers
May 21-25 in San Diego, California.

Called the Secretary-Treasurers conference, the 5-day event will cover various aspects of union and financial administration, election rules, and recordkeeping, and is designed to ensure compliance with federal regulation and internal union procedures. Instructors include ILWU attorneys, union staff, and International and local officers.

Each U.S. local and affiliate is invited to send two participants: its secretary-treasurer (or other officer in charge of finances and recordkeeping) and the office manager or other staff

person who maintains the union's financial and administrative records. Depending on the number of official participants, space may be available for a limited number of trustees selected

by their local union. Only individuals nominated by their local affiliate will be permitted to attend.

An official announcement has been sent to each local.

Participants may register online at
https://www.ilwu.org/2023-ilwu-secretary-treasurers-conference/

THE DEADLINE TO REGISTER IS APRIL 7TH.

Report back on the 73 Durban Strikes conference

It was an honor to represent Local 10 as one of 14 members to go to Durban, South Africa. Our mission was to learn about the 1973 Durban Strikes as well as be a part of a cultural exchange to build solidarity with members of South African labor organizations.

The conference started with scholars who were presenting papers that seemed out of touch with the working class. The papers were 100 percent research based and did not cite any workers who participated in the strikes. I found it odd that we were getting opinions and perspectives from people who weren't in the country during the strikes. On top of that, a lot of these presenters weren't even Black. In 1973, it was a Black workforce fighting for better wages.

On the second day, we had a great presenter who actually spoke on the build-up to the 1973 Strike. He spoke about how the strike actually began in the 1940's and continued into 1973. The struggle for justice continues to this day. The 1973 Strikes were powerful because the people risked everything in such an oppressive state when apartheid was at its height. Despite the repression, people still refused to work and fought for better wages.

The third day was much more relatable. We shared space and exchanged ideas with other workers like the RETUSA General Secretary Joseph Dube. The day started with a tour of the docks and surrounding areas. We learned about how thousands of workers were crammed into barracks and dispatched out to work for next-to-nothing wages. We also learned how the military extorted labor of prisoners to build the harbor. My biggest takeaway is that the tactics that may work in the U.S. are not the same tactics that will work in South Africa. We have to show solidarity with our South African comrades that allow for growth. We suggested ideas and offered solidarity. We also learned the importance of passing the torch and enable the youth to head the fight for an equitable future.

South African workers strike for better wages. With financial stability, I hope that our comrades can see one day that wages are not the only concern: workplace dignity and health conditions are just as valuable. Nepotism and the shape-up system still exist in South African ports. With workers making anywhere from \$5-\$20 per hour on average, it is hard to get all the workers on the same page and in the same fight. If workers resist or show any sign of opposition, they are blacklisted and only given minimal work or they are given the worst jobs like on docks that work coal. Jobs are run through a broker and not a worker-run dispatch hall, so the employer has all the power.

I am again thankful for this opportunity and hope that one day we can have global solidarity where we all have a fair piece of the pie.

Beau Logo, Local 10
Young Workers Committee Chair

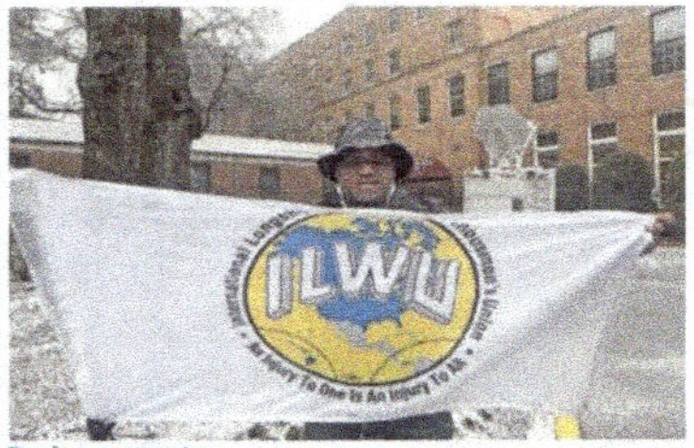

Paying respects: *Local 19 member Tyrone Harvey was on vacation when he heard about the killing of Tyre Nichols by police officers in Memphis, TN. Harvey headed to Memphis to attend the funeral and show solidarity from the ILWU. "I was on vacation and happened to turn on the news and saw the video of police officers beating Tyre Nichols. I immediately drove to Memphis to pay my respects. I attended the funeral that along with dignitaries, including Vice President Kamala Harris. I'm wondering when this police abuse is finally going to end," Harvey said. Harvey drove to Minneapolis to attend the funeral of George Floyd in 2020.*

Published by the International Longshore and Warehouse Union

THE DISPATCHER

www.ilwu.org

VOL 81, NO 2 • FEBRUARY 2023

The Local 10 solidarity delegation to Durban, South Africa included members and pensioners. They attended a conference marking the 50th anniversary of the Durban Strikes, visited the Port of Durban, and connected with local dockworkers and activists.

Port Envoy Gen. Stephen Lyons visits Tacoma page 2

Postmaster: Send address changes to The Dispatcher, 1188 Franklin St., San Francisco, CA 94109-6800.

Local 10 delegation marks 50th anniversary of the Durban Strikes

Wave of worker shutdowns revived anti-apartheid struggle in South Africa

More than a dozen members of ILWU Local 10 recently traveled to South Africa to learn about the country's incredible history, as well as to connect with dockers and other activists. They flew, by way of Johannesburg, to Durban on South Africa's Indian Ocean coast.

At the country's third largest city and most important port, they attended several conferences to commemorate the 50th anniversary of the "Durban Strikes," a massive wave of worker shutdowns that revived the struggle against apartheid and thereby changed the course of South African history. Strikes also have been central to the making of the

ILWU, from 1934 to 1948 and 1971-72, so attending events to remember and celebrate South African workers' power was too good an opportunity to ignore.

If Americans know of one person from South Africa, it is probably Nelson Mandela, a Black South African man imprisoned from 1964 to 1988, for fighting for racial equality. He, along with tens of millions of other South Africans of African and Asian descent, suffered under a brutal racial system called apartheid, which might be described as Jim Crow segregation on steroids. The long, hard, and noble struggle against apartheid made Mandela and many other South Africans heroes around the world. Black workers played a major role in fighting white supremacy in South Africa.

ILWU's historical ties to anti-apartheid struggle

On multiple occasions across three decades, members of ILWU Locals 10 and 34 as well as Local 6 and other ILWU locals supported the global struggle against apartheid. First in 1962, again in 1977, and most importantly, for 10 days in 1984, rank-and-file dockworkers refused to unload South African cargo in the Port of San Francisco. Bill Chester, then an ILWU International Vice President, was active, as was the Southern Africa Liberation Support Committee, a rank-and-file committee established inside Local 10, in 1976. Leo Robinson, Larry Wright, Charlie Jones, Billy Proctor, Leron "Ned" Ingram, Howard Keylor, Jack Heyman, Dave Stewart, and *continued on page 7*

☆ Honolulu, Hawaii

By S Scott

By S Scott

By S Scott

ALOHA: TO LOVE

By S Scott

By S Scott

By S Scott

By S Scott

By S Scott

By S Scott

By S Scott

By S Scott

By S Scot

By S Scott

By S Scott

By S Scott

"Since the beginning of history mankind has struggled individually and collectively for political, economic and cultural betterment and has found the greatest ability to make such advancement through democratic organization to achieve common aims.

"Therefore, we, who have the common objectives to advance the living standards of ourselves and our fellow workers everywhere in the world, to promote the general welfare of our nation and our communities, to banish racial and religious prejudice and discrimination, to strengthen democracy everywhere and achieve permanent peace in the world, do form ourselves into one, indivisible union....

Constitution of International Longshoremen & Warehousemen's Union

By S Scott

NOTES